Everything you need to know about

FORMULA 1 2023

MELVIN WEZENBERG

Copyright © 2023 Melvin Wezenberg

No part of this book may be reproduced or used in any manner without the prior written permission of the copyright owner, except for the use of brief quotations in a book review.

Dublin,
Ireland
2022

The views, information, or opinions expressed in this book are solely those of the author and do not represent those of their employers. The Author in any way whatsoever, cannot be responsible for your use of the information contained in or linked from this book. The author assumes no responsibility or liability for any errors or omissions in the content of this book. The information contained in this book is provided on an "as is" basis with no guarantees of completeness, accuracy, usefulness or timeliness.

If you like going a certain way, then be bold and do it.
Daniel Ricciardo

PROLOGUE

I'm honoured and thrilled to be writing my second book on Formula 1. After the adventure of *"Everything you need to know about Formula 1 2022"*, I am more motivated than ever to write the next pages you will be reading. I'd like to thank everyone who bought a copy of last year's edition of this book, and am happy to say that this year we will cover even more! The sport of Formula 1 is ever growing and this means there is so much to write about. While I will go over some of the more basic ideas of the sport as well to make sure this book is an asset for any new or old fan, we've got some spicy content ready for you that goes into quite a bit of detail of the sport. We have exclusive insights from questions I got to ask Zak Brown and Daniel Ricciardo at an event, as well as all the details on what happened with the driver market, rules, budget caps and even the future of the FIA.

The drama and controversy of last year's season were not forgotten in the paddock this year, and while the rivalry between Ferrari and Red Bull were far from the tensions of last year, we can gather interesting pieces for what I will predict will the most exciting season of the decade:

The Formula 1 2023 season.

Enjoy,
M

CHAPTER 0: FORMULA 101

A BRIEF OVERVIEW OF THE BASICS

It's the pinnacle of motorsport. The best 20 drivers from all over the world come together to battle it out across six different continents. On average, a driver dies every single year, making it one of the most dangerous sports in the world. Every time a driver enters their multi-million race car, they know the risk, the adrenaline and the pride that comes with the job. This chapter, will explain everything you need to know about the sport, whether you have been watching for years or haven't seen a single race, you can use this chapter to work up your foundational knowledge of Formula 1.

The sport started over 70 years ago, back in 1950, with cars that don't even look remotely the same as the majestic formula 1 cars that we know today. The very first season saw 81 different drivers compete, with 31 different teams throughout the season! While the amount of drivers and teams that participated was higher than the last decades, the number of races, 7, was far fewer than what we know today. Technology, especially mechanical technology, was new and improving rapidly, but while the cars lacked the modern tweaks that we see in today's cars, they were anything but slow. The cars that took place in the first ever Formula 1 race, in Silverstone in Britain, were far more rapid than any luxury car you can buy today. For the statistics geeks amongst us, the very first cars racing in Formula 1 could accelerate from 0 to

100 km/h in less than 4.0 seconds and could reach top speeds of 290 km/h. In comparison, the 2022 Lamborghini Huracan, takes 3 seconds to go from 0 to 100 and has a top speed of 325 km/h. That's 72 years later! While cars were already extremely fast, it would still take a long time before they started focusing on safety. The sport's dangerous image came to a peak during the 1994 San Marino Grand Prix. This weekend's grand prix was seen as one of the darkest days in sports, and we've since never heard of a sport where multiple casualties happened on two consecutive days. Racing, back in those days, was done without necessary safety measures such as the infamous "halo", tech-pro barriers and in some cases, even seat belts. During the tragic weekend on which the San Marino Grand Prix took place, the talented Roland Ratzenberger unfortunately passed away in a crash during qualifying, and not even 24 hours later, the world-famous Ayrton Senna, died during the race. Luckily, this weekend shook up the sports organisational body and racers, and the safety of the drivers, fans and pit-teams have increased significantly. The changes in technology and safety measures meant that the sport has gone through some major changes which have resulted in several different "eras" of the sport. Each change came with new rules and adaptations, and depending on how well teams were able to adapt and anticipate to the rule changes, the pecking order of the teams would change. This brings us up to the last couple of years of Formula 1, which consists of 10 teams, each competing only with 2 drivers. Since 2016, a total of 20 men have entered the Formula 1 races and have fought to be crowned the winner of the Formula 1 Drivers Championship. Historically, only men have been racing in Formula 1, but we're seeing

multiple women climb the ranks of the sport in the likes of the W Series, Formula 3 and Formula Renault. It may not be all too long before we see a woman entering the top tier of motorsport.

In the last decade, we have raced in two different Eras: the Hybrid Era, and the post-hybrid Era, which we entered this year. The hybrid era saw a dominance of Mercedes like we haven't seen before in the sport. How this dominance came to be, and what influenced the team to perform so well, will be explained later in the book. For now, let's cover the ten teams that are currently competing in Formula 1 in alphabetical order (number of constructor championships won in brackets):

1. Alfa Romeo (0)*
2. Alpha Tauri (0)
3. Alpine (Renault) (2)
4. Aston Martin (0)
5. Ferarri (16)
6. Haas (0)
7. McLaren (8)
8. Mercedes (8)
9. Red Bull (6)
10. Williams (9)

*Alfa Romeo won between 1950 and 1953 but the constructors championship was not an official price yet.

As mentioned before, like in most sports, there have been several era's of supremacy by certain teams. You can compare it to Real Madrid winning the Champions League three years in a row between 2016 and 2018, or Nadal winning the French Open 5 years in a row. The latest dominances have been held by Red Bull (2010-2014) and Mercedes (2014-2021). In 2021, Mercedes' dominance was challenged by Red Bull, resulting in Max Verstappen winning the championship over Lewis Hamilton in the final laps of the final race. Mercedes took home the constructors title, but felt devastated as their winning momentum seemed to be disappearing. Some other details to know about the teams in F1 is that Ferrari holds an honorary spot in the sport. To imagine Formula One without Ferrari would be like imagining Major League Baseball without the New York Yankees. Ferrari is the sport's most prestigious team, having been there since the beginning and having won the most races and championships, by far. Thanks to this, Ferrari tends to get a couple of extra benefits that other teams do not get and beyond that most drivers dream to drive for Ferrari at some point in their careers, regardless of the current performance of Ferrari.

Formula 1 is owned by the Liberty Media Corporation and generates a net income of over 1.4 billion dollars every year. That money gets split 50-50 between the competing F1 Teams and the Formula 1 Group. There are two championships happening in an F1 Season; The Drivers Championship and the Constructors (Teams) championships. Only the constructor's championship provides price money, while the driver's championship is for honour. Last year Red

Bull (1st place) earned over 700 million dollars while Ferrari (2nd place) "only" earned 165 million. The FIA can be seen as the FIFA in Football or the ITF in Tennis, and is the governing body of the sport as they update rules. Teams in F1 can also be punished for any rule breaks that may occur throughout a season. In the 2020 season, one of the teams had clearly copied the car off another team and therefore breached the rules. They were punished by the FIA and race stewards and lost half of their points earned throughout the season. The FIA oversees the race stewards, which are like the referees of Formula 1. The race steward is responsible for overseeing the race and ensuring that the rules and regulations are followed. The race steward will also be tasked with dealing with any incidents that occur during the race and making sure that the race is conducted in a safe and fair manner. The race steward will work closely with the FIA and race control in order to ensure that the race is conducted in accordance with the rules and regulations set out by the FIA. The FIA race steward for 2023 has not yet been announced.

Now let's create a quick team sheet to help you understand all important characters in F1.

Formula One Group President: Stefano Domenicali
FIA President: Mohammed Ben Sulayem

Red Bull Racing: Christian Horner **(Team Boss)**,
Max Verstappen **(Driver)**,
Sergio Perez **(Driver)**,
Daniel Ricciardo **(Reserve Driver)**

Scuderia Ferarri: Frédéric Vasseur **(Team Boss)**,
Charles Leclerc **(Driver)**,
Carlos Sainz **(Driver)**,
Antonio Giovinazzi **(Reserve Driver)**

Mercedes AMG: Toto Wolff **(Team Boss)**,
Lewis Hamilton **(Driver)**,
George Russel **(Driver)**
Mick Schumacher **(Reserve Driver)**

Alpine F1 Team: Otmar Szafnauer **(Team Boss)**,
Estaban Ocon **(Driver)**
Pierre Gasly **(Driver)**
2023 Reserve Driver TBD

McLaren: Żak Brown **(Team Owner)**,
Andrea Stella **(Team Principal)**
Lando Norris **(Driver)**,
Oscar Piastri **(Driver)**,
Alex Palou **(Reserve Driver)**

Alfa Romeo: Andreas Seidl **(Team Boss)**
Valtteri Bottas **(Driver)**,
Zhou Guanyu **(Driver)**,
Robert Kubica **(Reserve Driver)**,
Antonio Giovinazzi **(Reserve Driver)**

Aston Martin: Lawrence Stroll **(Team Owner)**
Mike Krack **(Team Boss)**
Fernando Alonso **(Driver)**

Lance Stroll **(Driver)**
Stoffel Vandoorne **(Reserve Driver)**

Haas: Gene Haas **(Team Owner)**
Guenther Steiner **(Team Principal)**
Nico Hülkenberg **(Driver)**
Kevin Magnussen **(Driver)**
2023 Reserve Driver TBD

Alpha Tauri: Franz Tost **(Team Principal)**
Nyck De Vries **(Driver)**
Yuki Tsunoda **(Driver)**
Liam Lawson **(Reserve Driver)**

Williams: TBD **(Team Principal)**
Logan Sargeant **(Driver)**
Alex Albon **(Driver)**
Jack Atiken **(Reserve Driver)**

A lot of these names you will be reading above may not be names you know, or even the names you had expected to read. What is known as Silly Season in Formula 1, the time of the year where a lot of drivers contracts are discussed, kicked off just after the summer this year and caused a lot of drivers to switch teams. In Mid-December, we unexpectedly saw a Silly Season for Team Principals take place when, within 1 week, we saw Williams, McLaren, Ferrari and Alfa Romeo change their Team Principals or Team Boss but we will discuss this in more detail later in the book.

RULES AND REGULATIONS

Before going over the events of last season, let's go over the rules and regulations. A big part of the 2022 season were the new regulations that came into play. However, let's first start with some of the basics. A standard Formula 1 weekend consists of three days but how these three days look like depends on the race format that is being held each weekend. Throughout the 2022 season we saw three weekends using a Sprint Race Format but in 2023 there will be 6. However, to keep it simple, we will focus on how a classic race weekend looks like and what rules are applied to on each day of the weekend.

THURSDAY

The weekend officially starts on Thursday with driver and team interviews and some teams also do a traditional track walk. It is mandatory, unless the driver has asked for an exception, to attend the press conference for each driver during a slot of 45 minutes on this day. Before the start of the weekend each driver also has to already make a tire selection for the entire weekend. While each driver gets plenty of Inter and Wet tires for the whole weekend, the drivers have to pick 10 sets off slick tires. Choosing your tire split correctly before the weekend can be a first step to winning a race for a driver. Most weekends teams tend to choose around 4-6 sets of soft tires 2-4 sets of medium tires and 2-4 sets of hard tires. Once you have used a set in practice or qualifying, the tires will be worn and will not perform as well during a race.

FRIDAY

On Friday, teams have two Free Practices (FP1 and FP2) to optimise their car set up and prepare for the coming race. You may think, why can't they just find one good set up and leave it for the rest of the season? Well, some tracks have a lot of straight lines and require a high top speed of the car. Other tracks have a huge amount of sharp turns and require the car to steer quick, smooth, and consistent. Since each track has their own characteristics, the teams need to adjust their cars slightly to optimise their lap times. The two sessions provide a perfect opportunity for teams to fine-tune their machines and ensure they have the perfect balance of power and handling. Although there are certain limitations on tire changes and pit-lane safety during these practices, teams are free to experiment with different components and strategies. At the end of each Free Practice session, drivers can try a practice start, allowing them to get to grips with the track conditions and refine their technique ahead of the race. Data such as lap times, fuel consumption, tyre pressures and other important factors can be monitored in real-time, allowing teams to make small adjustments to improve their performance. This technology has become even more important with the introduction of more advanced aerodynamic packages and tighter rules on engine performance. By using data analysis, teams can better optimize their setups to maximize their performance on race day. Teams do not have to use the same engine in Free Practice as in the race. The Monaco Grand Prix is the only race that has a different practice schedule, with FP1 and FP2 taking place on Thursday instead of Friday. On Friday the track is open for tourists to visit and for the Royal Family to rest. The rest of the weekend still follows the same schedule, with qualifying and the race taking place on Saturday and Sunday respectively. Finally, teams also use the practice sessions to familiarize themselves with the track and gain a better understanding of the unique characteristics of each circuit. This can be especially important on new or unfamiliar tracks, as teams must quickly adapt their setup and driving style to suit the conditions. Teams are also allowed to use test drivers in the practice sessions, enabling them to get a better idea of how different drivers perform in the same car. By taking advantage of the practice sessions, teams can ensure they are fully prepared for the race ahead. Each Free Practice lasts 60 minutes and cars can use any and all components on Friday, without any obligations to use these in qualifying or in the race.

SATURDAY

Before we get into the more complex rules that must be adhered to on Saturday, or Qualifying Day, it is important to understand a few things about the engines used in Formula 1. The Hybrid Era, which began in 2014, saw the switch from V8 to V6 Hybrid engines. This marked the introduction of several engine modes, ranging from a standard race mode used for optimum battery harvesting, to a qualifying mode with maximum revs and more aggressive ignition timing. Although the latter is great for setting a quick qualifying time, it would be too risky to put such strain on the engine for 72 laps in a race. This is why teams must carefully assess their engine modes, as they affect not only engine life, but also reliability and fuel. Typically there are several – up to nine – modes in between the two extremes. Now that we have discussed the engine piece, let's look at Saturday. Saturday is a critical day for Formula 1 teams, as this is when they must set their qualifying time. During FP3, drivers prepare for the qualifying session, scouring for that perfect setup to set a blistering time. It's a race against the clock as teams must find that perfect setup before the qualifying starts, as no changes can be made to the car after FP3, besides small repairs. After FP3, the first major moment of the weekend comes in the form of qualifying, a three-stage knock out system (Q1, Q2, Q3) lasting 18, 15, and 12 minutes respectively. In each stage, the five slowest cars are eliminated until the top 10 starting order is determined at the end of Q3.

The hours after qualifying consist of a frenzied period of activity as cars are hurriedly moved from and to their garages and subjected to scrutineering checks. To work on an F1 crew during this time is to work under immense pressure, as teams have only three and a half hours to inspect, prepare, and possibly repair the car that has been pushed to its limit in qualifying. After the three and a half hours are over, teams enter into a period known as Parc Fermé. This is a French term used across motor sports, meaning that cars are literally 'sealed' for a certain time period, with limited modifications allowed overnight. It's a moment of high tension as teams race against the clock, ensuring their cars are fully prepared and legal for the race ahead. With all the regulations, engine modes, and scrutineering checks in mind, it's truly a test of skill, determination, and wit. Teams must stay focused and have an eye for detail if they want to take the chequered flag at the end of the weekend. When we talk about sealing the car, some teams literally do this by throwing a wrapping around the car. There are very strict 22 subclauses that cover what is allowed to be changed during this period so here they are summarised in 11 quick bullet points. (These are simplified of course, the actual rules have a lot of technical details included)

1. Teams are allowed to start engines;
2. dd or remove fuel and fit a fuel breather
3. Remove wheels
4. Take out the spark plugs to better inspect the engine
5. Fit the cooling fans or fit heaters
6. Fit a jump battery to access and test electronic systems
7. Bled brakes and drain engine oil
8. Adjust the front wing angle
9. Adjust wing mirrors, pedals and seat belts
10. Fill up the driver's drink bottle
11. Repair of genuine accident damage (under the watch of an assigned scrutineer)

SUNDAY

Sunday in Formula 1 is race day - the most important of the weekend, with teams vying for championship points. After the Parc Fermé rules from Saturday, we enter the pre-race stage, where cars may be allowed one or two out-laps, allowing engineers to make small repairs if necessary. Two minutes before the start of the race, the cars will do a "Formation Lap", driving at any pace but without overtaking. Because of this rule, the pace of this formation lap is largely determined by the polesitter and can vary quite a lot from race to race. Once the Formation Lap is completed, the starting light sequence will culminate, with five lights turning on in sequence until all 5 lights turn off to signal the start of the race. During the race there are a lot of rules and sanctions that can follow a rule break, probably too many too mention and keep this book under 1,000 pages. Hence the most common ones are mentioned here:

- Jumping the start (5-second time penalty or drive-through penalty)
- Exceeding the speed limit during a safety car period (5-second time penalty or drive-through penalty)
- Reversing in the pit lane (10-second time penalty or drive-through penalty)
- Ignoring double-waved yellow flags (5-second time penalty)
- Causing a collision with another driver (5, 10 or 15-second time penalty)
- Exceeding the maximum number of engines or power unit components used (5-place grid drop)
- Exceeding the pit lane speed limit (5-second time penalty or drive-through penalty)
- Ignoring blue flags (5-second time penalty or drive-through penalty)
- Ignoring track limits (5-second time penalty or drive-through penalty)

There are many different punishments for breaking the rules of Formula One. These three are the most common:

Drive-Through Penalty: A driver must drive through the pit lane within three laps.

Time Penalty: A driver gets a 5, 10 or 15 second penalty. That means at the next pitstop the car has to be fully stopped for this amount of time. If there are no pitstops left, this time will be added from the finishing time.

Grid Penalty: A driver gets a penalty that contains the number of spots he drops in the grid. If this is during the race he will have to give back these positions, if this is before or after a race this will happen at the starting grid of the first upcoming race.

Upon finishing the race points get handed out to the top 10 drivers.

1st Place: 25 points
2nd Place: 18 points
3rd Place: 15 points
4th Place: 12 points
5th Place: 10 points
6th Place: 8 points
7th Place: 6 points
8th Place: 4 points
9th Place: 2 points
10th Place: 1 point

If the leader has completed more than two laps but less than 75% of the original race distance, **and is red flagged to end the race,** the above shown will be halved. If less than two laps are driven, no points will be awarded, and if more than 75% of original race distance is driven full points will be awarded. If drivers finish tied on points the positions get decided on results (first most wins, then most 2nd places, etc). Any driver can change teams during the season. In this case, his or her points with the previous team get added to his Drivers' points tally. But, the Constructors' points tally goes to the respective teams.

POST-RACE PARC FERMÉ

At the end of the weekend, after the race has finished and most viewers are tuned out, the cars that finish the race must again go into Parc Fermé. At this point they will get checked by the scrutineers again and until everything has been properly checked the stewards can still decided to change any finishing classification. In 2021, the FIA added a rule that after every race one car at random will get checked and may stay under Parc Fermé until much later in the evening for more detailed checks.

Budget Cap

Now that the rules of the weekend are clear, let's move on to some specifics that we saw in the 2022 season, and that are likely to be a big part of the 2023 season. The first very interesting thing that we saw in the 2022 season of Formula 1 is the budget cap. As of the 2021 season we had had a budget cap for each team that limited the spending. This meant that the smaller teams have more of a chance to compete against the larger teams since the differences in spending were limited by the budget cap. In the past the top three teams (Ferrari, Mercedes and Red Bull) have had a lot more resources that they could apply. The budget cap for 2021 was set at 145 million USD, which is slightly below the average team spending like Alpine prior to 2021 but far beyond the budget of Haas. Resources are not directly in correlation with the performance of a team, however it is likely that a team that has higher resources has a bigger R&D department and therefore is more likely to develop their car better than their competitors. One thing that is important to mention for this budget cap is that the salary of the drivers are not included. Hence, the bigger teams are still more likely to be able to snatch the better drivers as they can pay more salary to the drivers. If you have been watching the 2022 Season, you've probably heard a lot about this budget cap, so let's break down what happened. Red Bull was found to have breached Formula 1's $145 million budget cap by 1.6%, even when taking into account an unclaimed tax credit. As a result, the FIA issued them a $7 million fine, as well as a 10% reduction in their Restricted Wind Tunnel Testing and Restricted Computational Fluid Dynamics (CFD) limits. They are also obligated to cover the costs incurred by the FIA's Cost Cap Administration during their investigation, and are subject to an automatic referral to the Cost Cap Adjudication Panel should they not follow the punishments given. Despite this, the FIA found no evidence that the team or any of its key figures had acted in bad faith or attempted to conceal the breach, which they considered to be minor given it was less than 5% of the budget threshold. This breach of the budget cap is likely to have a significant impact on teams for the upcoming season. Red Bull Racing may find themselves at a competitive disadvantage due to the financial and performance-related penalties imposed by the FIA. To remain competitive in the face of budget restrictions they will be forced to look for more cost-effective solutions, or may find themselves having to make sacrifices in terms of personnel or resources in order to stay within the budget cap. Additionally, the FIA's Cost Cap Adjudication Panel may impose additional sanctions on teams found to have breached the budget cap, further limiting their competitive edge.

CHAPTER 1: WHAT HAPPENED IN 2022?

A lot happened in 2022. We started the season in anticipation of the results of the new rules and regulations. First of all, the size of the tyres increased, in comparison to the 2021 season. The rim size increased to 18 inches (45.7cm), which in simple English means that the tyres should be more sensitive to changes of direction. It also means that any historical data on how long a tyre lasts before it will burst or becomes significantly slow, is no longer valid. This means that at every track, teams have to start from scratch to figure out what the best tire strategies are for the weekend. If you have been watching this season at all, you will know that not all teams were on top of their tire strategy this year, which could be a result from this change. Another change that happened in the rules was the design of the Formula 1 car. All teams get a very detailed set of rules that must be followed when they design their car. The rules for this year (and the years to follow until at least 2026), made sure that the cars were designed in a way to minimise disruption of airflow, which means that the cars are more capable of following each other at close proximity without losing speed. Already on the first day of 2022 pre-season testing we were able to see impact of the changes in the car designs. The biggest change noticeable was related to the ground-effect that the 2022 cars had. As the name suggests, the ground-effect is a design of the car's floor that sucks the car to the ground by sucking the air underneath the car, instead of pushing it over the car. All teams did a great job at sucking the air under the car, but what a lot of teams were not able to spot in their design is that at top speeds the car came so close to the ground that the airflow stopped and forced the car to bounce back up. The repetition of sucking the car down and bouncing back up again was given the name porpoising and quickly became a big problem for many of the teams. A combination of the tyre changes, car changes and porpoising problems meant that it was going to be anybody's guess at the pecking order that we would see in the 2022 Formula 1 Season. The 2022 season was split between testing in Barcelona and Bahrain, each test lasting three days. While testing is always a bit of a mystery in terms of seeing who is doing well and who is not, early signs pointed towards Red Bull and Ferrari looking very strong, while Mercedes seemed to have an uncontrollable car. At the first race of the season, in Bahrain, qualifying concluded the true performance of each of the team's cars and gave us a good idea what to expect for the season. The storylines of the 2022 season were: Red Bull vs Ferrari, Mercedes' tumultuous season, McLaren vs Alpine and The Battle of the Bottom.

Red Bull vs Ferrari

The sun shone brightly over the desert track as the anticipation of the fans reached fever pitch. It had been years since Ferrari had a car that could compete for the championship, and now, with Charles Leclerc taking pole position, it seemed like their dreams were about to come true. Red Bull, with Sergio Perez and Max Verstappen, were not far behind, and the qualifying results had set the stage for a thrilling season ahead. As the lights went out for the first race of the new 2022 season, the battle between the four drivers began. Ferrari and Red Bull were neck and neck, and it was anyone's guess who was going to win this race. Max and Charles swapped positions multiple times, pushing each other to their limits and displaying some of the most amazing driving seen in Formula 1 in years. There was a noticeable difference between this year's battle and the one seen in previous the season; the team radios to the FIA and race leads were silent and no action was taken that could endanger the drivers, or the race. It was obvious that there was a lot of mutual respect between Max, Charles, Checo and Carlos as the overtakes were daring, but never over the limit. The pace between the two teams seemed to be almost the exact same throughout the race. During some laps, it seemed it was the Bulls that had the upper hand, but then a couple of laps later, Ferrari would show the power of the Prancing Horse. As Max and Charles showed their on-track battle skills, the crowd watched in awe as the race continued. When the race neared its conclusion, disaster struck. Both Red Bull cars suffered from fuel flow problems and had to retire from the race. It was a heartbreaking moment for the team, but the drivers didn't let it dampen their spirits. It was thus Charles Leclerc who was the first to see the chequered flag and emerge victorious, but it was clear that the battle for the championship between the two teams was just beginning. Ferrari had beaten Red Bull and taken the win, but even in defeat, the Red Bull drivers were seen smiling and cracking jokes with their rivals. It was a sign of respect and camaraderie that had become rare in the 2021 season, but would be persistent in 2022. Not even a week later, we had moved on from Bahrain to Saudi Arabia for the 2nd race of the season. All eyes were on the championship battle between Max Verstappen and Charles Leclerc, and who would come out on top. Qualifying was intense, and it was a huge surprise when neither Max nor Charles but Sergio Perez took pole position. He had put in an incredible lap, beating his Red Bull teammate and the Ferraris by just 0.2 seconds. The race was a nail-biter as various safety cars came into play, and the drivers had to use their strategies wisely. Verstappen was the most fortunate, as he was able to pit under the safety car restrictions and moved up to first place. On the other hand, Perez was not so lucky and ended up in fourth place. When the chequered flag was waved, it signalled the end of a thrilling race. Max Verstappen and Charles Leclerc both left for the next race with 1 win each, setting up an exciting championship battle for the next race.

After a small break, and a voyage around the world, Formula 1 headed into their third race of the season in Australia. Australia had been missing from the Formula 1 calendar for a couple of years due to Covid-19, and had since also done some changes to its track. This meant teams still had little to no knowledge of how their car would perform in the upside-down. Red Bull needed to show that they could be reliable and consistently competitive in order to keep their title hopes alive. The team worked hard to fix the issues with their car to make sure that they could be competitive. When the race weekend came around, the Red Bull team was determined to show their strength and speed. Charles once again won pole position, with Max and Perez behind him. As the lights went out at the start of the race, Max jumped ahead of Charles and the two lead drivers engaged in spectacular racing. The results of the race would leave a bitter taste in the mouths of the Red Bull team. After a promising start, they had been unable to capitalise on their superior speed due to the car reliability issues. It was a crushing blow for them to see their car failure throwing away an almost certain victory, and their hopes of a true championship challenge were starting to slip away. Max again did not finish the race due to technical problems, while Perez finished 2nd to save some points for the team. Luckily for Red Bull, this would be the last race that caused reliability issues, and from here on out, it was Ferrari that would face difficulties of their own. In the ensuing races, the tussle between Red Bull and Ferrari was like a game of cat and mouse, with the lead jumping back and forth wildly. Similarly, Max Verstappen and Charles Leclerc engaged in a thrilling battle for supremacy. As the season progressed, both teams seemed to be pulling away from the pack with a kaleidoscopic array of colors. Then came the Monaco Grand Prix, where Sergio Perez clinched an incredible pole position in the dying moments of qualifying, only to crash out in the very same lap. An accident, or a strategy to avoid letting anyone finish their qualifying lap? We'll come back to this later, as this moment would be become a major issue in the Red Bull Team. This race also marked the beginning of Ferrari's downward trend, as Red Bull surged ahead in the points chart.

Red Bull's performance outshone Ferrari for the second half of the 2022 Formula 1 season due to a combination of race strategy, driver errors and team tactics. Red Bull's divergent development strategy, prioritising weight loss, enabled them to gain an advantage that Ferrari could not match. Ferrari's development strategy of chasing aerodynamic gains proved less successful, leading to a number of avoidable driver errors that Red Bull was quick to capitalise on. By the time the Azerbaijan Grand Prix arrived, Red Bull had already built a substantial lead in the Constructors' Championship, with Ferrari lagging behind by 97 points. At the Azerbaijan Grand Prix, Charles Leclerc had the lead, but Red Bull's Max Verstappen soon overtook him and went on to win the race. Even with some weird set backs for Verstappen, such as not having enough fuel in qualifying in Singapore, the rest of the season seemed to go from bad to worse for Ferrari with Max Verstappen putting in a 6 race win streak and Ferrari only being able to win 4 races in the entire year. What started so promising, was followed by a repeated story in which Red Bull finished first and Ferrari would finish 2nd, this happened 8 times throughout the season.

The season saw a historic moment when Max Verstappen was crowned World Champion after only 18 races (out of 22) in 2022. Sadly for Max, his streak of drama-filled wins continued in 2022. This year, it happened at the Japanese GP, where there was so much confusion that even though Max won the title, he didn't get to celebrate until everything was confirmed at the US GP, two weeks later. The Japanese GP was initially delayed by an hour due to torrential rain. After the race finally got going, the drivers only completed 28 of the 53 laps due to the time constraints. Everyone assumed that since the race was incomplete, only partial points would be awarded. However, much to their surprise, Max was awarded full points and declared the World Champion. It turns out that the FIA had a rule in place that stated that if the race restarted after a red flag and at least two laps were completed, even if the race was stopped before the full distance, full points were still awarded. Even the likes of Christian Horner weren't sure if the rules were correctly followed, and so a proper celebration of winning the title wasn't done until the US GP, two weeks later.

As for Red Bull, and the Constructors Championship, they were able to win it in the same US GP, allowing the team and Max to celebrate double. Ferrari was disappointed to lose the championship, but they congratulated Red Bull on their victory. Christian Horner said that it was a true testament to the team's hard work and dedication that they were able to come out on top. The victory was made even more special by the fact that Red Bull had managed to dethrone Mercedes AMG Petronas F1 Team, who had held the Constructors Championship for the past eight seasons. This was an impressive feat, and it highlighted the team's impressive performance throughout the season.

MERCEDES

The 2022 season for Mercedes in Formula 1 was a tumultuous one. Despite having a decade of dominance in the world's fastest motorsport, Mercedes was unable to win a single race at the start of the season. This was a crushing blow for Lewis Hamilton, who was coming off a record eighth Formula One championship and was on the verge of his first winless season. It was already apparent in the pre-season of the 2022 season that neither George nor Lewis were able to drive consistent lap times in their new 2022 Mercedes. The main problem that Mercedes was facing this year was the porpoising of their car. Their W13 car seemed to bounce around the track way more than any of the other cars on track. At one point, the bouncing got so bad that Lewis Hamilton was seen exiting the car after a race in Azerbaijan looking like he was in pure agony and had attained some injuries to his back. The team's top speed was also lacking, and seemed to be problematic as the car wasn't able to overtake during any of the races. It wasn't all too rare that because of their lack of top speed that the silver arrows had to start the race from further down the grid. The lowest point of the season occurred in Saudi Arabia when Hamilton was unable to progress through Q1 of qualifying. It also seemed as if the loss of last season likely had an impact on the performance of Hamilton in the first half of the season. However, despite enduring a difficult start to the season, Hamilton was able to turn things around in the second half of the season and regained his place as a true world champion level driver. The dynamics between Russell and Hamilton were fascinating to watch throughout the season. Despite being a formidable rival, Russell and Hamilton have shown a great deal of respect for each other on and off the track. Russell admitted that their dynamic could have been different had Mercedes had a more competitive car in 2022. The team was a great pair to watch as they just wanted to deliver a win for the team, regardless of who the driver was to do so. The second half of the season was an impressive turn around for Mercedes, as they didn't only improve the performance of their car, but also started to become a threat to Ferrari. In the final 11 races of the season Mercedes scored 278 points in comparison to the 251 points that Ferrari scored and almost caught up with the Prancing Horses. To add to this, while Ferrari wasn't able to win a race since Austria (race 11), Mercedes won their latest race in Brazil (Race 21) and only had three races in the second half of the season in which they didn't score a podium. It's probably fair to say that the momentum going into next season is with Mercedes and not with Ferrari.

In conclusion, the 2022 season was a challenging one for Mercedes in Formula 1, but they were able to battle through it with the help of George Russell and Lewis Hamilton's performance. They made a good team in 2022 but it will be interesting to see how the dynamic changes if they both have a chance to fight for the title.

McLaren vs Alpine

McLaren and Alpine, it's a storyline that we've been looking at more often in the last years of Formula 1. In fact, it was probably the rivalry between these two giants that made the Netflix show "Drive to Survive" such a success in its first season. This year was no different, as the two teams have been engaged in a fierce battle all season long, vying to be the 4th best team at the end of the season.

The battle began at the start of the season, with Alpine looking to finally overcome McLaren and take the number 4 spot in the standings. Alpine had a strong start to the season. Team Principal Otmar Szafnauer joined the team in 2022, and despite having yet to win as team principal, he had put together a strong and competitive team as the shareholders of Renault were looking for the team to compete with the giants of the sport. McLaren, on the other hand, had been a powerhouse in Formula 1 for years, and with Andreas Seidl at the helm, they looked to continue their improvements and strong performance rise from the last couple of years. With Daniel and Lando as their drivers, the team believed they had the strongest lineup on the grid, and wanted to give them the best cars on the grid too.

The season was a true rollercoaster for both teams, with extreme highs but also worrying lows. It was Alpine that saw a superb start of the season, collecting 16 points in the first two races, while McLaren collected only 8. The next couple of races were a shock for Alpine as the young talent Lando

Norris showed some spectacular skills and pushed the team to 59 points by the 7th race of the season, Monaco. Alpine seemed to lack an answer to his skills, and remained behind with only 40 points. The team could have probably been even further ahead if the performance of Daniel Ricciardo was at par with his teammate, but the gap between the two teammates seemed to only grow. During the Monaco GP, Lando Norris even lapped his teammate, and left the team with a hard decision on whether they wanted to continue working with Daniel Ricciardo. By Race 11, Alpine had made its comeback thanks to Estaban Ocon and Fernando Alonso both collecting a handful of points at each race. The teams were tied at 81 points after the Austrian GP, and went into the second half of the season neck and neck. The battle between the two teams came to a head at the Dutch and Belgian GPs, where McLaren was no match for the Alpine's in qualifying and during the race. Within two races, Alpine had extended its lead to McLaren by 24 points, but more importantly, they showed that they truly did have the superior car. With a bit of luck, McLaren still managed to overtake the French team at the Singapore GP but never looked like they would take the win to the end of the season. The season ended in Abu Dhabi with Alpine achieving 173 points, while McLaren ended up at 159. Neither teams came truly close to their overall goal, to compete with the top three teams. In fact, if the teams would have combined their point count, they still wouldn't have beaten Mercedes for third place.

The Battle of the Bottom

While a lot of Formula 1 fans probably only focus on the top drivers and top teams, some interesting developments were also happening at the bottom of the standings. There was only one team that wasn't participating in the race for the bottom spots, as it was the historic name of Williams that was 10th and last place with only 8 points. However, the teams of Alfa Romeo, Haas, Aston Martin and Alpha Tauri were fighting to get as high in the team standings as possible. Initially, it looked like the winner of these 4 teams would be Alfa Romeo. They got star driver Valtteri Bottas to join their team, and he immediately proved to be worth the money. With the car being extremely strong in qualifying, and fast enough to hold back other cars during the race, the teams rose quickly to capture 59 points in 9 races. At this point, they were in the race with McLaren and Alpine for 4th place! Unfortunately, it wasn't all rainbows and butterflies for the Swiss team. Alfa Romeo performed extremely poorly in the second half of the 2022 Formula 1 season due to a number of issues. The most significant was a lack of reliability. Alfa Romeo suffered from a number of mechanical issues during this period, with engine and power unit failures being particularly common. This caused numerous retirements and put the team at a disadvantage in comparison to other teams. In addition, Alfa Romeo's lack of performance upgrades in the second half of the season also hindered their ability to compete at the front. The team had been unable to develop their car during the first half of the season due to the new regulations, and this lack of development work continued into the second half. This meant that their car was not able to keep up with the pace of development of the other teams, and they were unable to make any significant improvements. The 51 points that the team had gained in the first 9 races, only grew to 55 by the end of the season, which wasn't enough to compete with Alpine and McLaren, and put them in the cross-hairs of Aston Martin, a team that only had 16 points by race 9.

Unlike Alfa Romeo, Aston Martin had a remarkable second half of the 2022 Formula 1 season, thanks to a combination of factors. Firstly, their driver line-up proved to be a potent combination. Sebastian Vettel and Lance Stroll drove with a confidence and passion that was beyond compare, working in tandem like two pistons in a race engine. Vettel's racecraft and experience and Stroll's raw speed were a deadly combination, and the two drivers pushed each other to new heights. In addition, Aston Martin had made some significant technical improvements to their car in the second half of the season. These improvements were like a new set of wings, giving the car a new level of performance and allowing them to fly around the track. The team's upgrades didn't just increase their speed but especially allowed them to keep their tyres in good shape during the races, and to conserve fuel during the longer stints. Finally, the team had also benefited from some favourable race conditions in the second half of the season. On a number of occasions, Aston Martin had been able to take advantage of wet or mixed conditions to score points, as their car seemed to thrive in these conditions. Throughout these last races of the season, they were able to have an incredible comeback and tie with Alfa Romeo on points at the final race of the season, with Alfa Romeo winning due to the count back rule. The countback rule in Formula 1 is a method of determining the final classification of a race when two or more drivers or teams have the same number of points. It is based on the number of first-place finishes each driver has in the season. The driver with the highest number of first-place finishes will be ranked higher than the other driver(s). If both drivers have the same number of first-place finishes, the driver with the most second-place finishes will be ranked higher, and so on down the list. Therefore, it was thanks to Valtteri Bottas' P5 at the Emilia Romagna Grand Prix earlier in the season that P6 in the constructors standings went the way of Alfa Romeo.

Finally, let's talk about Haas and Alpha Tauri. Haas and Alpha Tauri both had moments of excellence and moments of disaster, resulting in a mixed result in terms of points. Both teams had experienced drivers on their roster, with Haas having Kevin Magnussen and Alpha Tauri having Pierre Gasly. Both drivers had experienced significant success during their careers, and this provided both teams with an experienced core that they could rely on. However, both teams also had drivers who were relatively inexperienced. Haas had Mick Schumacher, while Alpha Tauri had Yuki Tsunoda. While both drivers had shown promise, their lack of experience often led to mistakes that cost the teams points and even some high bills to pay. In addition, both teams had experienced a number of technical issues during the season. Haas struggled with reliability issues on their car, while Alpha Tauri had experienced a number of power unit failures. These technical issues prevented both teams from scoring as many points as they would have liked, and contributed to their moments of disaster. Finally, both teams were also affected by the new regulations. Haas usually does a lot of their car developments through outsourcing parties, and since the rules and regulations were completely new this year, it was hard for them to get the details right. Alpha Tauri historically used the older Red Bull car to base their cars off. However, since again the rules were completely new, they couldn't use a previous Red Bull car, and they had to design their car on their own. The teams ended up in 8th and 9th but thanks to the rules staying relatively similar in next years season, we can expect some big upgrades coming the way of Haas and Alpha Tauri.

CHAPTER 2: SILLY SEASON

A lot of things happened that makes this year particularly interesting when looking at the drivers market. There were internal conflicts at some teams, other teams even went so far as to buy out a driver of their contract, and there were contract disputes over who a driver belonged to. In this chapter, we'll take a look at all the drivers, which teams they driver for and what has happened this year that makes the situation so interesting. Let's start with arguably the driver that set off a chain of events when he announced that he would be retiring from Formula 1 after the 2022 season. His name?

Sebastian Vettel

Sebastian Vettel is a German racing driver who was, until last season, competing in Formula One for Aston Martin. He is a four-time World Champion, having won the championship in 2010, 2011, 2012 and 2013 with Red Bull Racing. He is widely regarded as one of the greatest drivers in the history of the sport. Vettel began his career in Formula One with Sauber in 2007, before moving to Red Bull Racing in 2009. In 2010, at 23 years and 134 days, Vettel became the youngest ever driver to win the World Championship, and followed this up with victories in 2011, 2012 and 2013. After his success at Red Bull Racing, Vettel moved on to drive for Ferrari, where his ambitions of becoming a five time World

Page 37

Champion were tossed aside by the Mercedes dominance. Vettel couldn't make Ferrari world champions, and after years of 2nd and 3rd places, Ferrari decided to give the challenge to another driver, Charles Leclerc. This forced Vettel to find a seat elsewhere, and he found it at the newly entered Aston Martin. While Vettel still loved racing, the last couple of years he started being more and more involved with some important issues going on around the world. The biggest challenge he wanted to tackle, was that of climate change. This challenge, in addition to wanting to spend more time with his family, ultimately made him decide that the 2022 season would be the final season he would race in. At the age of 35, Vettel retires relatively early, and many drivers still feel like he may yet come back in the future. During the final race, Vettel was unable to score enough points to get Aston Martin to beat Alfa Romeo, but he did break the all-time record for most votes for Driver of the Day (56%). With the all time youngest World Champion leaving the sport, many fans felt a hole in their heart but it also left a hole in the team of Aston Martin, as they needed to find a driver to partner their young, rich and talented Lance Stroll. The replacement of Vettel would come in the form of another World Champion as Fernando Alonso announced that he would be joining Aston Martin in 2023. With one legend replacing the other, the driver market got a shock that nobody really saw coming and silly season had kicked off. The team of Aston Martin looked to have an incredibly strong lineup for the season to come and everyone is wondering how well their car will be.

Lance Stroll & Fernando Alonso

Lance Stroll is a Canadian racing driver, born in Montreal, Quebec, to Lawrence and Claire-Anne Stroll. His father is a billionaire entrepreneur, and his mother a former fashion model. Due to his family's fortune, many fans haven't taken Stroll too seriously in his first years in Formula 1, as they believed he bought his way into the sport. However, Stroll actually began karting at the age of eight, and won his first championship in 2008. He moved up the karting ranks, winning the Quebec championship in 2012. Soon after, he made his car racing debut in 2014, competing in the Formula Renault 2.0 Alps series. He won the championship in his maiden year, and also won the Toyota Racing Series in New Zealand. For someone who "bought" his way into the sport, he also seemed to have an incredible amount of talent. In 2015, Stroll made his Formula One debut as a test driver for the Williams team. He was promoted to a race seat for the 2017 season, and scored his first points with a 9th-place finish at the Monaco Grand Prix. When Vettel joined Stroll at Aston Martin, many fans were surprised that Stroll could actually match the pace of Vettel, a 4 time world champion. While Vettel scored more points in both seasons the two shared as teammates, the gap between the two drivers was relatively small compared to some other teammates in the sport. Lance Stroll will continue to race for Aston Martin the next years, alongside his newest teammate, Fernando Alonso.

Fernando Alonso is a name that almost everyone will know. Alonso is a two-time World Champion, having won the titles in 2005 and 2006. In 2001, Alonso made his Formula 1 debut with the Minardi team. He scored his first point in his third race with the team. After having finished 1st, 2nd and third for a huge number of years in the world championships across a variety of teams, Alonso announced his retirement from Formula 1 at the end of the 2018 season. Luckily for the fans, he announced his comeback to the sport in 2021 and joined Alpine (Renault) alongside the French Driver Esteban Ocon. Unfortunately, Renault had overpromised their car to Fernando Alonso, and while the car at times was blistering fast, it was unreliable and Alonso was never able to challenge any of the top teams. Thus, when he heard that Vettel was retiring, Alonso made the decision to switch teams and give it a try with Aston Martin. Beyond the lack of performance of the car, Alonso was fed up with the team of Alpine, including his teammate Ocon, whom he had fought with on track several times throughout the season. While Aston Martin hasn't been able to perform as well as Renault in the 2022 season, it seems like there are some strong developments going on at Aston Martin that could make them challenge for 4th place in 2023. Only time will tell if Alonso made the right call. So what did Alpine do after Alonso left? Alonso, didn't just leave Alpine, but he left the team at a very crucial timing that had quite a significant impact on some of the contract negotiations that were going on. Vettel's retirement took everyone by surprise, and Alonso's move followed quickly after Vettel, adding in yet another surprise. Well, here's where things get very juicy.

Oscar Piastri

Almost all teams in Formula 1 these days have a youth driver academy, which allows younger drivers to get guidance from big teams while they are still competing in the lower racing levels. This is an excellent system for the drivers, as well as their teams as they can easily replace older drivers or unsuccessful drivers with new and young potential. Oscar Piastri was the youth driver of Renault/Alpine and had been a reserve driver for the team in 2022. Oscar Piastri, an Australian super talent, was winning races across all of the divisions he was competing in and was an obvious choice to replace Fernando Alonso. However, as previously mentioned, the timing of Alonso's departure was a bit inconvenient. On August 1st 2022, Alonso officially announced that he would be joining Aston Martin. This date was coincidentally also the date that was on the release clause of Oscar Piastri's contract. In simple, non-legal, terms: Oscar Piastri's contract could automatically be turned into a Formula 1 contract up until July 31st 2022, without Oscar Piastri having to sign anything. Hence, when Alonso announced his leave Alpine quickly followed with a statement sharing that Oscar Piastri would join the French team as the replacement of Alonso. Chaos began when only a couple of hours later, Oscar Piastri shared with the world that this statement was not correct, and that he would not be driving for Alpine. Oscar Piastri was indeed correct as the clause of his contract had expired and he was now free to sign with whomever he wanted. The announcement that he would join McLaren finally came after a long discussion with the FIA and sports regulators agreed that Oscar was free to go. This left Alpine with yet another hole in their team. While the team had a couple of drivers they wanted in their team, the situation was complex as other teams were also fishing for drivers, and some of the targets Alpine wanted were even bound by contract to other teams. Luckily for them, Alex Albon had to miss a race weekend due to appendicitis. His replacement for the weekend, would be the change they needed to secure a great driver for the next season.

Nyck De Vries

Since Albon's appendicitis was unpredictable, Williams had to quickly act and find a replacement for their driver. The only reserve driver out there that weekend was Mercedes Reserve Driver Nyck De Vries, a Formula 2 and Formula E world champion. Nyck had to jump into the Williams Formula 1 car for an hour of practice, and get straight into qualifying. To the surprise of everyone, he managed to advance to Q2 and qualify 13th, ahead of his Williams teammate Nicholas Latifi. Jumping into a Formula 1 car and driving at its full speed is incredibly difficult, out qualifying a teammate who has been doing this for several seasons is nearly impossible. The next day in the race, Nyck de Vries managed to finish 9th and score 2 points for the team. In the entire 2022 season, Williams was only able to score 8 points (2 De Vries, 2 Latifi, 4 Albon). The impressive performance of Nyck De Vries, and his quick adaptation to the Williams car, made him a very popular driver choice for all the teams that were still looking for another driver for their 2023 lineup. After a couple of weeks of conversations with teams such as

Williams, Alpine and Alpha Tauri, Nyck made the decision to sign for Alpha Tauri. This was an interesting sign because Alpha Tauri already had 2 drivers contracted to them in 2023. Thus, it meant one of the drivers was free to go to the team that he had expressed interest in joining.

Pierre Gasly

Pierre Gasly is a French Formula 1 driver that grew up competing with Max Verstappen, Charles Leclerc and Jules Bianchi. Especially the third name is a name that is very important to Pierre Gasly as he saw Jules as a brother, and was devastated when Jules passed away in the Japanese Grand Prix in 2015. Two years later, Pierre Gasly joined Formula 1 as a driver for Toro Rosso (now Alpha Tauri) and took a lot of inspiration from the way Jules lived his life. He proved to be an amazing driver and in 2019 he got the opportunity to drive for one of the title challenging teams, Red Bull Racing. Unfortunately, it seemed that driving for a top team with only two years of experience was a lot to handle for Gasly. His performance dropped so significantly when he joined Red Bull that he was only allowed to race half a season for the team before being transferred back to Alpha Tauri. Since then Gasly has performed incredibly well and even managed to win his first Formula 1 race with Alpha Tauri. His performance has been steady, but since a return to Red Bull was unlikely, the Frenchman realised that he may have to look elsewhere if he ever wants to compete for a championship team again. Partly thanks to his nationality, he started looking at Alpine. Alpine, having lost Alonso and Piastri, was desperate to find their second driver. The company, is partially owned by the French state, which made it very appealing for the team to have two French drivers in the team. Thanks to Alpha Tauri also being open to this, and Nick De Vries being a very interesting sign for the team, Gasly was let go from his contract and able to sign for Alpine. Gasly wasn't the only driver on the grid that was let go from his contract prematurely though, at McLaren a similar situation was unfolding.

Daniel Ricciardo

Daniel Ricciardo. The big smile of Formula 1. His charisma, his flair and his positive energy make him a very popular driver across the Formula 1 teams. His journey started at the age of 14, when he left Australia to take a more serious approach to racing. He moved over to Europe and quickly made a great name for himself, and entered Formula 1 with the HRT team. After a year of racing at the back of the grid, he then went on to join Toro Rosso for 2 years until he replaced Mark Webber at Red Bull Racing. His four years at Red Bull were extremely impressive, out-competing Sebastian Vettel and Max Verstappen in every season. However, in 2018 it became obvious to the Australian talent that Red Bull was investing their future into Max Verstappen, giving him a better pay and designing the car more around the Dutchman. This was a sign for Daniel Ricciardo that it was time to leave the team and continue his adventures somewhere else. He spent 2 seasons with Renault, delivering the team a podium finish, which resulted in the team boss Cyril Abiteboul getting a tattoo of Daniel Ricciardo's nickname "The Honeybadger". He made a surprising announcement when he decided to join McLaren in 2021. However, at McLaren the great performance of Daniel was nowhere to be found as he was repeatedly beaten by his younger teammate Lando Norris. Despite Daniel winning the grand prix of Monza, McLaren was not satisfied with his performance and decided to buy him out of his contract. This is something that rarely ever happens in Formula 1, and hence must have been quite a hit to Daniel's confidence. None of the other teams could arrange a deal with Daniel either, which meant that the Australian will be participating the 2023 season as Red Bull's reserve driver. It seems like this deal between Red Bull has some hidden clauses as Ricciardo has repeatedly mentioned that he feels quite confident that he will be back on the grid with a winning car in 2024. Will that be Red Bull? Or maybe Mercedes? Either way, it seems like we haven't seen the last of Daniel Ricciardo yet.

Beyond this game of musical chairs, lots of things happened to the drivers that remained in their current team. We also saw some new drivers enter the market, so let's take some time to analyse the remaining drivers of the 2022 and 2023 season, starting with the most famous name in all of Formula 1 history.

Mick Schumacher

For those new to the sport- Yes, you read that correctly! But I'm not talking about Michael Schumacher. Instead, let's talk about his son, Mick Schumacher. He entered Formula 1 two years ago for the American team Haas. At first, it seemed like Mick was living up to his dad's name, as he outcompeted his teammate Mazepin. Unfortunately for Mick though, Mazepin did not compete in the 2022 season, due to his ties with Russia and Vladimir Putin. Haas decided to return to one of their former drivers, Kevin Magnussen. K-Mag, as some may refer to him, is a seasoned Formula 1 driver that is known for his cutting edge guts and his incredible pace. It didn't even take him one race to prove this to everyone, as he not only out qualified Mick Schumacher, but finished 5th in Bahrain. Meanwhile, Mick finished just outside the points in 11th place. The rest of the season didn't go much better for Mick in comparison to Kevin Magnussen. After 22 races, when the season closed in Abu Dhabi, Magnussen had managed to score double the points of Mick. In addition, Mick had racked up quite a bill for Haas by crashing in numerous occasions. The combination of these two factors meant that Kevin Magnussen's contract was extended by another year, while Mick's was not. Instead, another German driver was chosen to replace the famous name. Before we move on to the replacement of Mick, it is worthy to note that the relationship between Haas and Schumacher was definitely not one that ended on a high note. When Schumacher did his goodbye donuts at the end of the season, his team ordered him to stop. No other messages of goodbye or thanks were shared with Mick, which would be the customary thing to do in the sport. Hence, it's unlikely Mick will be returning to the sport through Haas, if ever. A more likely approach will be through the team of Mercedes, as he will become the 2023 reserve driver for the team. If history says anything about the reserve driver of Mercedes, things look very positive for Schumacher. Their two previous reserve drivers all got to race for a Formula 1 team in the next year; Nyck De Vries for Alpha Tauri and Estaban Ocon for Alpine.

Nico Hülkenberg

Nico Hülkenberg is a man that has had an incredible journey with countless ups and downs in Formula 1 so far. His career started all the way back in 2010 for the infamous Williams team. It was a season filled with spins, crashes and disappointment but also of a pole position and great talent for Williams and Hülkenberg. Unfortunately, it wasn't enough to convince the team to give him another season, which meant that Nico had to search elsewhere. After a year as reserve driver for Force India (now Aston Martin), he went back and forth between Force India, Sauber and Renault until 2020, when his 8-year streak in Formula 1 ended. The next two years, it seemed like there wouldn't be another opportunity for Nico anymore to get back into the sport. While he got to make a couple of appearances thanks to COVID cases, no team was impressed enough to offer him a permanent spot as a driver on the team. It came as a surprise to many that Haas announced that he would be returning to the sport for the American team. To Haas however, it was no surprise as they had tried 2 younger, less experienced drivers without successes and decided it was time to have a team of experienced drivers, to get the team successful results in 2023.

Max Verstappen &
Sergio "Checo" Perez

If I would have finished my book a little bit earlier, I probably wouldn't have even considered giving this driving pair a single page in this book. Luckily for me, I didn't finish this book earlier though, and there is actually plenty to talk about. Max Verstappen & Sergio Perez entered their second season as teammates in 2022. In 2021, it could be argued that Max was only able to win his 2021 Driver Championship thanks to the help of Sergio Perez in the final race in Abu Dhabi. Based on that story, the couple seems like a perfect match as teammates. As we entered the 2022 season, that sentiment didn't really change. Verstappen was the first driver and won the majority (a record) of races throughout the season, but whenever he had an off day or his car would be in trouble, Perez would step up to challenge the win of the race. Red Bull decided relatively early in the season already that Perez would continue to be Max's teammate for 2023 and all seemed well in the world. Until, out of nowhere, it seemed like there had been friction in team Red Bull all along. In a race, where neither Max nor Sergio looked anywhere close to be competing for a win, the underlying tension suddenly showed its true colours. Max, who had already won the drivers championship and beaten the record for most wins in a season, was asked to let Sergio by in the final lap, in order to compete with Charles Leclerc for second place in the drivers championship. Max's reply, which could be heard on TV was *"I told you already last time, you guys, don't ask that again to me. Okay? Are we clear about that? I gave my reasons and I stand by it."*. So to recap: Max refused to help the guy who had helped him secure 2 championship (ok fair enough, one more than the other) at a moment where Max had absolutely nothing to lose. Why would he do that? Well, as it turns out Max was still pissed about something that had happened way earlier in the season, and it wouldn't be Formula 1 if it didn't have something to do with Monaco.

Charles Leclerc & Carlos Sainz

Charles Leclerc and Carlos Sainz are two of the most successful Formula 1 drivers of their generation, and both of them have found a home at Ferrari. The two drivers have a unique relationship, one that is based on mutual respect and competition.

Charles Leclerc began his professional career with Sauber in 2018, and it was not long before he made a name for himself. By the end of that season, he had finished in the top ten of the Driver's Championship and had earned himself the title of 'best rookie'. His impressive performance earned him a promotion to Ferrari for the 2019 season, where he quickly established himself as one of the fastest drivers on the grid.

Carlos Sainz had a more circuitous route to Ferrari. He initially joined the Toro Rosso team in 2015 and then moved to Renault in 2017. After two seasons there, he was promoted to McLaren for the 2019 season. His impressive performances for McLaren led to a move to Ferrari for the 2020 season, where he paired up with Leclerc to form one of the most competitive driver lineups on the grid.

The relationship between Leclerc and Sainz is one of mutual respect and competition. While Leclerc is the established leader of the team, Sainz has also made a positive impression in his first season with Ferrari. He has been able to take advantage of Leclerc's driving style and use it to his own advantage, making progress in areas where Leclerc had the edge.

Both drivers have very different driving styles, with Leclerc being more livewire and Sainz being more analytical. This can lead to divergent set-up strategies and development philosophies, but it also means they each put the car on the limit in different ways, showing up characteristics that might otherwise be hidden. This combination of Leclerc's livewire driving style and Sainz's analytical approach means that Ferrari has an incredibly well-balanced driver lineup.

Leclerc was the more consistent Ferrari driver in 2022, but Sainz was able to make significant progress in the second half of the season, outqualifying Leclerc in four out of the last six races. This progress has been noticed by the team, who recognize the importance of the two drivers working together and complementing each other's strengths.Ferrari's racing director Laurent Mekies has praised the "high-quality feedback" from both drivers, as well as their "drive to push the team to recover." He also commended the mutual respect and desire to work together that Leclerc and Sainz have shown.

The partnership between Leclerc and Sainz is an important part of Ferrari's rebuilding process. With both drivers pushing each other to their limits, Ferrari has the chance to become a title-winning force once again. This is a rare opportunity for both drivers to prove themselves and show the world what they are capable of. With the right combination of talent, respect, and hard work, Leclerc and Sainz could be the perfect formula for Ferrari's return to the top.

Lewis Hamilton &
George Russel

Lewis Hamilton and George Russel are two of the most daring and dynamic drivers in the Formula One circuit. Lewis Hamilton, the five-time world champion, is known for his lightning-fast reflexes and ability to pull off impossible passes with ease. The British driver is also renowned for his all-or-nothing attitude and never-say-die spirit that have seen him come from behind to win multiple races. Off the track, he's known for his infectious personality, sense of humour and love of fashion. George Russel is a young gun who's already making a big name for himself in the sport. His driving style is fearless and daring, and he's willing to take risks that others wouldn't dare. He's a master at navigating tight corners and often puts other drivers in his dust. Off the track, George is known for his cool, calm demeanour and his infectious laugh. Both drivers are fierce competitors and display an unwavering commitment to excellence. But while they're both on the same track, Lewis and George are always looking for ways to out-race each other.

Estaban Ocon

Estaban Ocon will remain at Alpine in 2021, where he will be joined by Pierre Gasly. In 2013, Ocon was signed by the Lotus F1 Team as a development driver, and he was given his first Formula One test with the team later that year. In 2014, Ocon moved up to the GP3 Series and won the championship in his rookie season, earning him a promotion to the GP2 Series the following year. In 2016, Ocon was signed by the Manor Racing Team and made his Formula One debut at the Belgian Grand Prix. Ocon has made a name for himself in Formula One with his aggressive yet consistent driving style. He has achieved several podiums and points finishes throughout his career, and has also become known for his ability to overtake other cars on-track. The French driver's story is a true rags-to-riches tale. He comes from a poor background but has worked hard to become one of the best drivers in the world. He is a great example of how anyone can achieve their dreams if they're willing to work hard for it. He's currently one of the few drivers that has earned his spot solely for his ability to drive his car, not due to any sponsorship that he brings.

Alex Albon & Logan Sargeant

Williams is set to have an exciting driver lineup for the 2023 Formula 1 season, with Logan Sargeant and Alexander Albon at the helm. Logan Sargeant is a 21-year-old racing driver from Fort Lauderdale, Florida. He currently lives in the heart of London and was the last driver of the season to sign for a team. Logan moved to Europe to pursue his dream of competing in Formula One. Logan recently became the first American to win a Formula Two race when he scored a victory at Silverstone. Prior to joining Williams, he has competed in three years of the FIA Formula 3 championship and has taken six podiums. He also won at Russia's Sochi Autodrom and narrowly missed out on the 2020 championship title. He will be replacing Nicholas Latifi at Williams and will look to bring his experience and talent to the team. Alexander Albon, on the other hand, will be entering his second season in the sport and is hoping to build on the potential he showed during his debut season. With Sargeant joining the team, Albon will have the opportunity to push himself and the team further.

Williams is looking to have a competitive season in 2023 and these two drivers will be integral in making that happen.

With their ambition, talent, and experience, the team hopes to make a name for themselves on the grid and show the world what they are capable of.

Valtteri Bottas & Zhou Guanyu

Valtteri Bottas and Zhou Guanyu are two well known names in the world of Formula One racing. They are both drivers that have potential to be some of the best on the track, but seem to lack consistency and fighting mentality. Valtteri Bottas is a Finnish racer who is known for his consistency on track and his amazing qualifying runs. He has a calm, cool demeanor that makes him a great teammate as well, and his ability to stay focused and composed under pressure has earned him the respect of his peers. He is also known for his meticulous race preparation, which has often resulted in podiums. If he starts on pole, he's likely to win the race to, but overtaking is not one of his strong suits. Zhou Guanyu is an up-and-coming Chinese driver who has been in Formula 1 for only a short time. His racing style is very technical and analytical, and he often uses his natural ability to anticipate the moves of the other drivers on the track. Off the track, Zhou is a bit of a jokester and loves to have a laugh with his fellow drivers. Zhou has mentioned that Valtteri is a true mentor to him and the duo seem to have a good relationship, as they are both trying to score as many points as possible for the team. Unlike other teams, there seems to be not a lot of tension between the drivers which is good for the constructors points.

Yuki Tsunoda

Yuki Tsunoda was born in Tokyo, Japan, on the 24th of March 2000. As a child, Yuki was a bit of a daredevil. When he wasn't busy playing video games, he was often found racing around the streets on his bicycle, or participating in whatever sport he could find. Yuki's parents were very supportive of his motor-sport activities, so it was only natural for Yuki to pursue it professionally. Yuki began his professional racing career at the age of 15, competing in the Japanese Formula 4 championship. His talent and ambition were quickly noticed and he was soon signed up for the Formula 3 championship. After a successful year in Formula 3, Yuki was given the opportunity to race in the FIA Formula 2 championship. He finished the season in a strong fourth place, demonstrating his speed and skill behind the wheel. Yuki's style of racing is aggressive and daring. He's not afraid to take risks in order to gain an edge over his opponents. He's also known for his ability to push his car to its limits and sometimes over the limits. He's also known for his sense of humour, which he often uses to lighten the mood in the paddock. Yuki had an excellent rapport with engine manufacturer Honda, which certainly played a role in helping him secure his place in Formula 1, he has since showed he also has the raw talent to maintain his seat.

Lando Norris

Lando Norris is quickly making a name for himself as one of the brightest young stars in Formula One. The 20-year-old

Briton has been on an upward trajectory since joining McLaren in 2017, and he has already established himself as one of the top drivers in the sport. Norris has been a key part of McLaren's resurgence in the past two seasons, as the team has made an impressive improvement to become one of the top contenders in the championship. Norris's impressive driving skills and consistency have been the main driving force behind McLaren's success, as he has consistently been able to out-qualify and out-race his more experienced teammates. Norris has also shown a remarkable maturity and poise in the cockpit, and his aggressive yet controlled driving style has allowed him to stay out of trouble and capitalize on any opportunity that presents itself. His impressive performances have earned him a place as one of the most popular drivers on the Formula 1 grid, and he is now seen as a key part of McLaren's plans to challenge for the championship in 2023. Norris has also become a key part of McLaren's promotional activities, and his good-natured persona and positive attitude have made him one of the most popular drivers in the sport.

Mattia Binotto, Andreas Seidl & Frederic Vasseur

Right before the end of 2022, when we thought the season was all done and dusted, the Formula 1 world was shook up once again, this time with news of three major team principal changes in one week. Mattia Binotto, Andreas Seidl, and Frederic Vasseur have all been involved in a flurry of activity as Ferrari, Sauber, and McLaren have all shuffled their management in preparation for the 2023 season.

The news first broke when Ferrari announced that Mattia Binotto would be stepping down as team principal after 28 years with the Italian racing team. Soon after, it was revealed that Frederic Vasseur would be taking over the role, leaving his position as CEO and Team Principal of Sauber Alfa Romeo to join Scuderia Ferrari.

Vasseur is a highly-regarded figure in the lower formulas of racing, having won numerous titles and races with his own team in F2 and F3. He is also fluent in Italian, having previously worked with Sauber, an Italian-backed Swiss team. Perhaps most crucially, he has a strong relationship with Ferrari's star driver, Charles Leclerc. The two have previously worked together at Sauber, and Leclerc has expressed his optimism about the new team principal, this piece will be extremely interesting as Mattia never dared to call a first and second driver in the team. Maybe Vasseur, with the relationship he's had with Charles and the performance of Charles in the 2022 season, will officially make Charles the main driver of the team. This would be a huge blow to Carlos as he didn't sign with Ferrari to be their second driver.

The news of Vasseur's move triggered a series of other changes, with McLaren confirming that their team principal, Andreas Seidl, would be leaving to join Sauber as chief executive ahead of their Audi merger. Seidl's departure was believed to have been part of the plan for some time, as McLaren had always known that he would eventually move to Audi in 2025. However, his move was brought forward due to Vasseur's arrival at Ferrari.

Seidl's replacement at McLaren is Andrea Stella, who has been promoted from executive director to team principal. Stella is a former championship-winning engineer with Ferrari, having worked with Kimi Raikkonen in 2007. His appointment has caused some debate, with many questioning whether he is a dyed-in-the-wool McLaren person. However, McLaren are confident that he is a good choice for the role.

Jost Capito

Williams has been a powerhouse in Formula One racing since the 1970s, but the team has seen a decline in recent years. The team was purchased by US investment firm Dorilton Capital in 2020 and Jost Capito was appointed team principal and chief executive in 2021. He had a long and successful career in motorsport, including stints as director of Volkswagen Motorsport, director of Ford's Global Performance Vehicle Programs, CEO of Volkswagen Motorsport, and CEO of Porsche Motorsport. Capito had the difficult job of turning around Williams' fortunes, but was unable to do so in two years. Williams have now announced that Capito and technical director FX Demaison will be stepping aside before the 2023 Formula One season. He said in a statement that it was a "huge privilege" to lead Williams Racing for the last two seasons and that he looked forward to watching the team as it continued on its path to future success. The team will now be looking to appoint a new team principal and technical director to succeed Capito and Demaison, and to continue the process of reviving Williams Racing.

CHAPTER 3: LOOKING AHEAD TO 2023

Now that we're all caught up on what happened in 2022 and during the winter break, we can now move on to our analysis of what we can expect in 2023. There's a lot of new topics to discuss such as the new rules and regulations, the new track calendar and of course the performance expectations. We'll go ahead and tackle them one by one.

THE NEW TRACK CALENDAR

The new track calendar is going to have a bigger impact than simply having some new tracks to the already existing list of tracks. Something that a lot of fans don't realise is the difficulty of the operational scheduling of Formula 1. While the cars may be the stars of the show, they are only part of the equation. Behind the scenes, teams of highly skilled and experienced professionals are responsible for the operational logistics of Formula 1. This includes managing the complex logistics of the cars, equipment, technicians, personnel, and travel throughout the season. These logistics must be managed in a way that allows the team to be competitive and successful in the sport. Teams must ensure that they have the right parts and tools available when needed. This requires constant communication between the team and suppliers to ensure that parts and supplies are available when needed. In addition to managing the cars, teams must also manage the personnel and equipment necessary to compete in Formula 1. Formula 1 teams typically travel with a large inventory of spare parts for their cars. This includes everything from engines and transmissions to suspension components, brake pads, and even bodywork. The exact number of parts varies from team to team, but teams typically travel with hundreds of parts for each car. These parts are often stored in large containers, which are loaded onto the team's transporters and shipped to the race track. The parts are then unloaded and stored in the team's garage, ready to be used in the event of any mechanical failure. A team may choose to bring more spares to more difficult races such as the Monaco Grand Prix, as this is a more challenging track which enhances the chance of a damage. In addition to the spare parts carried by the team, Formula 1 teams also travel with a large amount of tools and equipment. This includes jacks, fuel tanks, and a variety of other specialised tools and machines. These are used to repair and maintain the cars during the race, and to prepare the cars for practice and qualifying sessions. This ensures that the team is always prepared for any unexpected mechanical issue, and can quickly repair any damage to their car or replace any worn or damaged parts. With all of these parts and tools, you can imagine that adding one or two tracks to the calendar is more complex and costly than it may seem. So let's take a look at which tracks are added this year and how it will impact teams.

Initially, the 2023 calendar included three new race venues; the Chinese Grand Prix, the Qatar Grand Prix and the Las Vegas Grand Prix. Due to COVID concerns in China, the

Chinese Grand Prix has been removed from the calendar since its announcement, leaving the calendar with only 2 new tracks. If these two new tracks were placed after the Miami GP and the Saudi Arabia Grand Prix, the two tracks probably would have had minimum impact on the teams. However, they were placed after Brazil and Japan, which are countries that aren't all that close to each other. Therefore, next to the additional 80,000 tons of CO_2 in 2023 that Formula 1 teams will have to be accountable for, the teams will also have to deal with the headache of the complex logistics and costs of these two races. Below you can find the full track list for 2023 (and as a bonus, the order of that Formula 1 Calendar could have used to decrease cost and CO_2 emissions by as much as 46%).

2023 Track list:

March 5	Bahrain	Sakhir
March 19	Saudi Arabia	Jeddah
April 2	Australia	Melbourne
April 30	Azerbaijan	Baku
May 7	USA	Miami
May 21	Italy	Imola
May 28	Monaco	Monaco
June 4	Spain	Barcelona
June 18	Canada	Montreal
July 2	Austria	Spielberg
July 9	United Kingdom	Silverstone
July 23	Hungary	Budapest
July 30	Belgium	Spa
August 27	Netherlands	Zandvoort
September 3	Italy	Monza
September 17	Singapore	Singapore
September 24	Japan	Suzuka
October 8	Qatar	Lusail
October 22	USA	Austin
October 29	Mexico	Mexico City
November 5	Brazil	Sao Paulo
November 18	USA	Las Vegas
November 26	UAE	Abu Dhabi

Total distance covered: 133,570km
(if teams do not fly back home in between races)

2023 Cost- and Eco- friendly version Track list(**Not used**):

March 5	Australia	Melbourne
March 19	Singapore	Singapore
April 2	Japan	Suzuka
April 30	Bahrain	Sakhir
May 7	UAE	Abu Dhabi
May 14	Saudi Arabia	Jeddah
May 21	Qatar	Lusail
May 28	Azerbaijan	Baku
June 2	Austria	Spielberg
June 9	Hungary	Budapest
June 18	Italy	Monza
June 23	Italy	Imola
July 2	Belgium	Spa
July 23	Netherlands	Zandvoort
July 30th	United Kingdom	Silverstone
August 27	Monaco	Monaco
September 3	Spain	Barcelona
September 18	Canada	Montreal
October 22	USA	Austin
October 29	USA	Las Vegas
November 5	Mexico	Mexico City
November 18	USA	Miami
November 29	Brazil	Sao Paulo

Total distance covered: 72,127km
(if teams do not fly back home in between races)

With the budget cap, which will be $135 million in 2023, smaller teams will at least not be as impacted as before, but the 2023 track calendar is definitely another challenge for teams to face while keeping their costs at a minimum. The bigger teams will have the money, but still need to be smart with their logistics as the budget cap is challenging. The tracks that are added are quite unique tracks too. Las Vegas will have one of the longest straights (and fewest corners) on the 2023 calendar, meaning that top speed will be critical for this city race. Meanwhile, Qatar's characteristics are looking quite the opposite as the track's fast corners require a high downforce level, making Qatar one of the most sensitive tracks of the year.

All in all, these new tracks will give a new twist to the 2023 season, both logistically and in the form of two completely different tracks to tackle while designing the 2023 cars.

RULES AND REGULATIONS

The 2023 Formula 1 season is set to be yet another major milestone in the history of the sport, with a number of new rule changes being introduced to reduce porpoising and bouncing, improve safety and increase competition. These new rules have the potential to have a significant impact on the performance of the cars and the way in which teams approach the sport. The most significant rule change in 2023 comes in the area of the floor of the cars. The FIA has mandated a 15mm height increase at the outer edge of the floor to reduce the ability of teams to run the edge of the floor closer to the track's surface and gain an aerodynamic advantage. This will likely require teams to build in additional stiffness to pass the necessary tests. Additionally, the number of holes required to measure conformity has been reduced from six to four, and changes have been made to the geometry of the floor's edge to ensure that the FIA's regulations are adhered to. We have seen in 2022 that increasing the height of the car will have an inverse relationship with the amount of bouncing due to porpoising. Hence, increasing the height of the cars should reduce the porpoising for every team, but it also means cars are probably going to have slower lap times than in 2022.

The front wing has also undergone some changes in the 2023 regulations, with the flap and endplate juncture being further restricted. This has effectively ruled out the complex design introduced by Mercedes at the Canadian Grand Prix, which was expected to offer more 'outwash' then was originally intended. However, teams will be given a little more freedom in terms of adjustability, with the flaps now able to have 40mm of adjustability rather than just 35mm. The fillet radius between the elements and the brackets that can be used has also been increased from 2mm to 4mm.

At the rear of the car, the height of the rear wing tethers will need to be mounted 60mm higher than in 2022. The mounting studs between the power unit and chassis, and the power unit and transmission, will now also require a tensile strength greater than 100kn. All of these changes are relatively small and unlikely to pose a big challenge for any of the teams, but they do stop any advantages gained by innovation from last season, and at the same time offer new room for innovation in the 2023 season.

The halo, aka the roll hoop, has also been subject to some changes in light of the Zhou Guanyu accident at the British Grand Prix, with the loads that it must sustain being increased. This will likely require some teams to redesign the halo structure, as the new regulations will require it to be able to sustain forces applied to it in a forward direction as well as the rearward forces it already had to achieve. Additionally, any parts constructed above a certain height must be able to withstand a 15g impact with the ground and be made from an abrasion resistant material.

The weight of the car is also set to come down a little, with the pre-2022 minimum starting target mass of 796kg being reinstated. However, the minimum weight of the power unit has increased, as some of the associated pipework will now be included within its perimeter. This specific rule is most likely to impact championship winning team Red Bull Racing, as they had the heaviest car at the beginning of the 2022 season. The fuel density check will also be stricter, so there is a smaller chance that team's can disobey the rules.

A less technical rule, but a fun rule for the audience is that the FIA has added a seventh camera position to the cars, including one to be fitted facing forward within the driver's helmet, something that has been met with universal praise. We saw the infamous "helmet cam" with a variety of drivers throughout the season, but now every driver will have one.

In conclusion, the new rule changes for the 2023 season have the potential to have a significant impact on the performance of the cars and the way in which teams approach the sport. The changes are designed to reduce porpoising and bouncing, improve safety, and increase competition, but only time will tell how much of an effect they will have on the sport. In addition to this, this year the FIA also announced the 2026 rules and regulations, and starting in 2023, teams will start working towards this, hence we will dive into these rule changes in the chapter "2026 is coming".

PERFORMANCE PREDICTIONS

Last year I was able to correctly predict the struggles of Mercedes and the rise of Ferrari, and I aim to use my crystal ball again this year to take a look into what next season will hold for us. Of course, there are some changes happening that make it hard to predict exactly who will be performing well and who will not, but ultimately I think I have a pretty good sense of who will perform well next season.

Let's get started with the top contenders for the constructors title. Ferrari arguably had the fastest car on the grid for most of the 2022 season, closely followed by Red Bull Racing. However, as we have covered in the previous chapters already, Ferrari has undergone yet another leadership change with Binotto leaving the team. It's difficult to say exactly how long it will take for performance to improve after a leadership change, as it can vary depending on a number of factors. In general, though, it may take several months to a year for the full effects of a leadership change to be seen in terms of improved performance. Before the improved performance, most teams see a dip in performance when leadership is changed (e.g. Twitter and Elon Musk) and mainly for this reason that I think Ferrari will have a difficult season next year. Realistically, it won't be difficult for them to compete with other teams than Red Bull and Mercedes, but difficult enough that they will not be able to compete for a top two spot. That leaves the title to be fought out between Mercedes and Red Bull. Both of these teams are equipped with drivers that want to prove that they are the best in their team. Mercedes and Red Bull carry a lot of momentum from last season. Mercedes' moral is at a peak thanks to the uplifting end of the season, which even included a powerful victory. Red Bull has never been closer to finishing 1 and 2 in the drivers championship while also securing the constructors championship, and they will be eager to try the same stunt in 2023. Momentum is a real phenomenon in sports, and it can have a significant impact on the outcome of a game or competition. It's argued that momentum can give a team or individual a psychological advantage, helping them to perform better and potentially leading to a string of wins. Hence, I expect both of these teams to be fighting at the top of the championship next season. We've learned from the past that Mercedes is always at its strongest after a tough race or season, so I expect them to start next season incredibly strong. What will be interesting, and I'm sure a determinant for the result of the season, is the driver's dynamics between the two teams. We've already covered the tension that came to the surface at the end of the 2022 season between Max and Checo, and if this tension hasn't been resolved by March 2023, it may lead to problems. Not to mention, Daniel Ricciardo as a reserve driver will absolutely add to the pressure for both drivers, as Daniel will be more than eager to replace either, should their season fall apart. As for Mercedes, it's gone a bit unnoticed but George Russel beat Lewis Hamilton by more than 35 points. Only Jenson Button and Nico Rosberg were able to beat Lewis Hamilton over a season once. The fact that George

Russel was able to do so in his first season at the silver arrows says a lot about the kind of driver he is. Furthermore, comments made by both drivers during interviews and over the radio, indicate that neither driver is looking to be the second driver of the team. The first couple of races are going to be key to establish the dominance in the team.

Moving on to the midfield, it's time to make a bold prediction: Aston Martin will finish fourth. While I'm sure many of you will disagree, I'm standing by this one! You may say, *"But Aston Martin were only seventh this season!"*. All the same, there are numerous reasons why I am so sure of their rise in performance. First of all, there is owner Lawrence Stroll, who is arguably one of the most successful businessmen in Canada. He's historically gained a lot of profits from his investments, and his latest and largest investment is Aston Martin. With the money and time he's invested in this team, he must be expecting some return on his investment at this point, and I reckon the team goals for 2023 are going to be a lot higher than previous years. Additionally, there is the move of Fernando Alonso. Alonso's move was quite surprising as Alpine is currently outcompeting Aston Martin by quite a lot. However, in interviews Alonso almost seemed to have zero doubts about Aston Martin and how they are going to be outcompeting Alpine and the rest of the midfield next year. Clearly, this team must have something under their sleeves. Following Aston Martin, McLaren will be joining the fight for 4th place. McLaren's team has seen a huge reboot since 2018 and have frequently been competing for podiums in the past two seasons. They have a great lineup of drivers, with Oscar

Piastri and Lando Norris, and their car has been constantly improving. With the support of their new engine supplier, Mercedes, McLaren has the potential to become a real contender for the 5th spot in the Constructors Championship, and a genuine challenger to any midfield team. With the right strategy and a bit of luck, who knows what could happen? Fighting the top three doesn't seem realistic for McLaren in the 2023 season, but if they keep their development and driver program up, they may yet see the constructors title land with them within the next 10 years.

Alpha Tauri are poised to make a big jump up the grid in 2023. After their somewhat poor season, the team now has access to the technology of the Red Bull Car, which was the constructors champion of 2022. This gives the team a huge advantage and the potential to compete more closely with McLaren and Aston Martin. The team also recruited a new driver who will be looking to make his mark. Nyck de Vries is a highly rated rookie, while Yuki Tsunoda will be looking to become the first Japanese driver to move up to Red Bull Racing. The Red Bull car gives Alpha Tauri the opportunity to be competitive from the outset. It's a proven race winner, and with the new regulations for 2023, the team will have plenty of time to develop the car and make it even faster.

Haas, Alpine, and Alfa Romeo are the teams that I expect will be jostling for the remaining spots in the rankings, though none of them will likely be able to unlock the speed to compete with the top 5 teams. It's unlikely that any of the three will be able to surprise the world with a sudden jump in the rankings, as they all face their own unique issues. Haas has been struggling to keep up with the ever-changing regulations and has had difficulty finding a consistent driver lineup. Alpine has yet to find a way to get their car up to the speed of their competitors, having only managed to score points in a few races, especially as they continue to struggle with the reliability of their power unit and cornering speeds. Alfa Romeo, meanwhile, has recently gone through a leadership change, which could potentially shake up the team's results in the future.

At the bottom of this list, I would put Williams. Since the departure of Sir Frank Williams in 2013, the team has been in a state of decline. They are currently last in the constructors' championship and have finished last three times in the last four years. It's not just the fact that they are last, though. It's the fact that they have been last for so long, and have made no progress in improving their position. They are now at a point where making a comeback is looking challenging. Williams has been struggling financially due to new ownership. While other top teams like Mercedes and Ferrari have billions of dollars to spend on their teams, Williams is a stand-alone company and thus cannot commit the same amount of money to its team. Furthermore, the team is also having difficulty in competing with other teams in terms of technology and innovation.

In summation, I think we can expect the end of next season's constructor championship to look something like this:

1. Mercedes / Red Bull
2. Red Bull / Mercedes
3. Ferrari
4. Aston Martin
5. McLaren
6. Alpine
7. Alpha Tauri
8. Alfa Romeo
9. Haas
10. Williams

CHAPTER 4: 2026 IS COMING

Audi has officially announced that it will enter Formula 1 as an engine supplier in 2026. This move is part of their strategy to transition away from combustion-engined cars to electric and sustainable power sources. This coincides with F1's revised engine regulations, which will bring a 100 percent sustainable fuel and increased use of electric power. Audi's entrance into F1 will mark the first time in more than a decade that a powertrain will be assembled in Germany.

The revised engine regulations have been designed to attract new power unit suppliers. Starting in 2026, the turbocharged 1.6-liter V-6 engines used in Formula 1 will run on a 100 percent sustainable fuel, while the electric portion of the hybrid powertrain will produce three times the power as today's setup. The MGU-K, which harvests kinetic energy and deploys electrical energy via the crankshaft, will see its output nearly triple to 350 kilowatts, or about 469 horsepower, boosting the total system output to well over 1000 horsepower. The MGU-H, which currently harvests heat energy via exhaust gases in the turbocharger and can deploy electrical energy to reduce turbo lag, will be removed from the F1 power unit in 2026. The increased reliance on electricity will see the amount of fuel used in a race drop from 100 kg to 70 kg, while the removal of the MGU-H, along with other measures, is intended to decrease costs.

Audi's entrance into F1 was made official with images of a Formula 1 car mocked up with Audi livery. However, this image should be taken with a grain of salt as it may not be indicative of what the actual Audi-powered F1 cars will look like during the 2026 season. Audi will not field its own team, but it will provide powertrains to at least one team. This team turned out to be Sauber (currently competing as Alfa Romeo), which also announced that its technical and commercial partnership with Alfa Romeo will end after the 2023 season.

In preparation for the 2026 season, Audi is currently focused on hiring personnel and sourcing the technical infrastructure and buildings needed to develop the power units. These components should be in place by the end of the year, giving Audi three years to prepare its power unit. With Porsche and Ford also said to be entering F1 as an engine supplier, potentially with Red Bull Racing, 2026 is set to be an important year for the biggest global motorsports series. This year, we saw Honda exit Formula 1 as an engine manufacturer, but not even 6 months later, they returned on the Red Bull Car as they announced they will continue to support the "red bull power trains". In simple terms, this means Honda is still heavily involved with the engine manufacturing and furthermore announced they would be interested in a full comeback in 2026.

Other teams that are likely to join Formula 1 in 2026 include BMW, Porsche, and Ford, which are reportedly on track to make a return to F1 in 2026. In addition to the teams, Formula 1 is also looking to add new countries to the mix. As for the drivers, expect to see some of the world's best behind the wheel. With the addition of these new teams, we may see more than 10 teams in Formula 1 in the future, and therefore we will likely see more space for drivers to join Formula 1 and compete at the highest level of motor sport.

BONUS CHAPTER:

FORMULA 1 HISTORY & MCLAREN INTERVIEW

SPECIAL MOMENTS IN FORMULA 1

Right, you are now completely up-to-date on everything you need to know about the Formula 1 season of 2023. An achievement that not many people will complete. However, as with any sport, history is also important. Hence, as a gift to you, here you can find a chapter that shares some pretty special stories that have happened throughout the history of Formula 1. Names like Senna, Nicki Lauda and James Hunt, are all names you should know about to prove you are a true Formula 1 fan. To get you as passionate about these stories as some of the most historic Formula 1 fans will be, they will be written in a novel-like fashion, so you can truly relive these moments (before you watch them on YouTube). Enjoy, and remember the sport is still creating new legends, records and memories every year- so enjoy!

Page 77

How It All Started

It's the year 1950. Credit cards, diet soda, and roll-on deodorant were all yet to be invented. Life moved at a slower pace, something we'll likely never get to experience again. But while life was moving slow, some things were moving very fast. At the prestigious British Grand Prix, the first of its kind for the world championship, 200,000 spectators gathered to witness a momentous occasion. King George VI, Queen Elizabeth, and the Earl & Countess of Mountbatten were all in attendance to honour the drivers. Raymond Mays also made a special announcement, revealing the BRM V16 to the British public. This car, funded by the government, was the first serious attempt to break the dominance of the Italians in grand prix racing. The race began with the expected dominance of the Alfa Romeos, with their drivers Farina, Fangio and Parnell leading the race. The British manufacturers were not faring well, as the two E-Type ERA's of Leslie Johnson and Tony Rolt were already out after only two laps. The battle for the lead remained close, with Farina only just managing to hang on to first ahead of Fangio. Fangio put on a late charge for the lead, but was forced to retire on lap 62 after colliding with a straw bale. This allowed Fagioli to take second, although Farina still took the chequered flag first. At the end of the race, Farina was the proud winner of the first world championship grand prix, with Fagioli and Parnell close behind. The dominance of the Alfa Romeos was obvious, and Farina was rewarded with the full array of points, as well as a £500 prize for his victory. The British Grand Prix marked a triumphant start to the world championship for Alfa Romeo, and the dream of the BRM V16 challenging them in future races.

The 1976 Season; James Hunt & Niki Lauda

The 1976 Formula One season began with Niki Lauda of Ferrari winning in Brazil and South Africa, with James Hunt of McLaren finishing second in both races. The rivalry started to heat up between Niki and James when James won in Spain, but the victory was taken away when the back of his car was deemed to be too wide. This resulted in tremendous disappointment for James, who was now facing a divorce from his wife Suzy after she had an affair with actor Richard Burton. Further victories were secured by Niki in Monaco and Belgium, while James's disqualification was overturned and his car was adjusted to fit the standards. Unfortunately, tragedy struck during the practice for the German Grand Prix, when an accident caused one of the racers to break his leg. Prior to the start of the race, Niki held a debate between the racers and racing officials, suggesting that the race should be canceled due to the dangerous weather conditions. While some joined the vote, the majority ruled that the race would continue. During the race, both Niki and James used rain tires, which had to be changed at the pit stop due to the track drying up quickly. However, on the third lap, a suspension in Niki's car broke, causing him to swerve off the track and crash into a wall, with the car becoming engulfed in flames. Two other cars hit him, and some racers ran to pull him out as he caught fire. He was taken to the hospital and treated for severe third-degree burns and toxic fumes in his lungs. During the next six weeks of recovery, Niki watched as James continued to race and earn points. Eventually, Niki made a return to the racetrack, who to continue his competition with James. Niki even mentioned that James was equally responsible for getting him back behind the wheel. James eventually won the season, by one point over Niki. However, Niki was still considered the victor due to his courage and determination in the face of adversity.

Senna VS Prost

In 1988, Senna joined the McLaren team as a teammate to Prost, a French driver. The two quickly developed conflict, which culminated in the 1989 San Marino Grand Prix. Both agreed not to pass each other in the opening corner, but Senna disregarded this agreement and overtook Prost. This led to growing animosity between the two drivers over the 1989 season. The climax of the season occurred during the 1989 Japanese Grand Prix, where Prost and Senna were competing for the championship title. Senna attempted to pass Prost but the two collided, which led to Prost leaving the race while Senna continued to win. However, Senna was later disqualified and Prost was declared the champion. This led to accusations from Senna that FIA president Jean-Marie Balestre had favoured Prost. Senna and Prost's rivalry continued throughout the 1990 and 1991 seasons, with Prost moving to Ferrari in 1990. This led to increased tension between the two, with Senna wishing to join Williams but being blocked due to a clause in Prost's contract. During a press conference in 1993, Senna called Prost a "coward". Later that year, Prost retired from Formula One. Senna's tragic death at the San Marino Grand Prix in 1994 came as a major shock to the world. Despite their on-track rivalry, Prost was a pallbearer at Senna's funeral and later commented that part of him had died that day. This shows the respect and admiration that the two drivers had for each other, and how their rivalry was not built on hatred but on a mutual understanding of the sport.

Schumacher

Michael Schumacher is an undisputed legend in the world of Formula 1 racing. He is a seven time World Champion and has an illustrious career that spans two decades. Throughout his career, Schumacher has had many incredible, controversial, and memorable moments. In 1993, Schumacher faced off against his rival Aryton Senna in Belgium and managed to pass him on the grass. This daring move showed his undeniable talent and dare as a driver. One of the most memorable and controversial moments came in 1994 at the Adelaide Grand Prix. Michael Schumacher was leading the race and Damon Hill was one point behind him. On the 36th lap, Schumacher clipped the wall and Hill attempted to overtake him. Knowing that he would be unable to finish the race, he then crashed into into Hill, taking himself out of the race but also damaging Hill's car in the process. Hill has since argued that Schumacher did this on purpose though he denies this. It was not the only time that Schumacher was accused of purposely crashing himself or others out of the race. However, in the same year he also had an incredibly impressive show of skill in the 1994 Spanish Grand Prix where he managed to take 2nd place whilst driving in 5th gear for the last 40 laps, due to his gearbox faltering. Schumacher also had an infamous win in 1998 at the British Grand Prix when he took advantage of a technical loophole and took his stop and go penalty in the pit lane during the final lap. The finish line extended across the pit lane, meaning that he won as he was sitting there. The rules have since changed to prevent this from happening again. His legacy as one of the all time greats of Formula 1 will live on forever, and his impact on the sport will be remembered for years to come.

Printed in Great Britain
by Amazon